The Little Red Networking Book
Women's Empowerment - 2nd Edition

Ordering Information: Quantity sales. Special discounts are available on quantity purchases by corporations, associations, non-profits and others. For details, contact the author using the following information.

Jackson HR & Administrative Services
Email: JacksonHRService@gmail.com
Website: www.jacksonhrservice.com

ISBN: 978-1-7353422-3-8

I0041111

The Little Red Networking Book & Strategy Planner
Women's Empowerment - 2nd Edition

Your Strategy Planner begins on Page 45
with its own table of contents that starts on page 43 for your convenience

Acknowledgements

*"Tremendous amounts of talent are being lost to our society
just because that talent wears a skirt."*
Shirley Chisholm

This edition is inspired by the women who mentor me from afar; Former First Lady Michelle Obama, Ms. Oprah Winfrey, Vice President Kamala Harris, and now Justice Ketanji Brown Jackson. The glass ceilings that you've broken continue to empower me not to settle for level average, but to push beyond good and aspire for greatness.

Thank you **to my Power Squad: My business coach, *Deshawn Bullard*; my career coach, *Rhonda Hight*; and my National WE Leadership Team *(Erica Harris, Mill Davis, Kedra Fairweather, Lawanda Griffin, Donna Tebought, Nickie Medlin, Jibrayah Marson, and Krisitann Walker*)** for your labor of love and support in what is now known as the "Networking In Red" event of the year, The Red Dress Brunch & Professional Development Retreat. Women will now know how to not only network but to make lasting, empowered connections and feel confident in doing so.

Networks are so important to what I do, and I would like to thank *Dunwoody High School Alum, West Georgia University Alum, Troy State University Alum, and the largest network of them all, The lovely ladies and Sorors of Delta Sigma Theta Sorority, Inc.*

To my Sistah Circle-Grown Folks Table Podcaster Co-Hosts *(Libby, Joyce, Delois, & Vickie)*, thank you for always stretching me, supporting me, mentoring me, and keeping me current on all things political and social.

Acknowledgements
Continued

I'm thankful **to the members of my congregation, *The Leadership Church in Metro Atlanta***, for their love and support in allowing me to be their Co-Pastor for these last twelve years. It has been my honor and privilege to birth a women's community out of what God called me to do for this church. I am a better leader because a small place called The Leadership Church is called to make a mega impact.

To my parents, *Talkoy and Anne Peoples*, thank you for your lifelong support, for being the first to buy a book, a shirt, or a ticket to any of my events, and also for making it easy to make you proud. I could not ask for better parents. I love you dearly.

To my brother, *Xavier Peoples* thank you for being a listening ear, a strong part of my network and always being available to support me.

Finally, I'm thankful **to my husband, *Tony Cash*,** The Financial Expert, My Daily Passion Pusher, and My Pastor. Thank you for being an advocate for women and women in ministry as well as for supporting me in creating a safe space for women and women's empowerment. I know that I am a Networking Expert now because of you. I am also thankful to my husband for *being my loudest and biggest cheerleader for success.*

And **to our children, *Kennedy and Jackson Cash*,** thank you for believing in me, encouraging me to keep moving women's empowerment forward, and your love, support and sacrifice.

Introduction

*I*n October of 2014, I began leading a women's empowerment weekend event as a community outreach networking program. The theme for the weekend was **"Moving from Comfort to Courageous."** I had a wonderful response from the community and continued to host a series of networking events for a diverse group of women in the community. My goal was to help women develop confidence in their spiritual walk and their femininity, as well as their dreams, goals, and aspirations.

Research shows that confident people are more attractive to their peers, have better jobs, are happier and are more productive than their less confident counterparts. Like most other things in life, developing confidence takes practice. I discovered that my networking events not only gave the women an opportunity to practice; it also gave me a chance to practice with developing relationships to obtain the support I needed to facilitate the programs. Little did I know, I was creating my own network.

When I made the decision to move confidently in faith to promote women's empowerment on the next level, I created a networking event called ***The Red Dress Brunch™*** in 2018. During this event, we acknowledge women's entrepreneurship and recognize women that empower other women in their communities, respective careers, and within the faith- based community. The event has grown to serve more than two hundred women annually and my network has grown exponentially as a result.

How was I able to achieve this growth? My experiences have shaped my belief that networking is much more than what people may believe that networking means. It's about connecting with someone on a level deeper than just exchanging phone numbers and email addresses.

I decided it was time to share my formula for building such a close knit community of connections and influencers that I can call upon to support my endeavors. You now hold that formula in your hands.

My Story

*W*hen I first became a business owner, I went to networking events just to collect cards. I would say "Hi, My name is Eleshia. Can I have your business card?" I thought this was how "networking" was supposed to work.

Unfortunately, many people have come to believe that networking is merely a mad dash to see how many business cards can be collected during the event. I discovered just how ineffective this activity turned out to be. I would send emails to the contacts I made and wouldn't receive replies. I would make phone calls as well, however I did so without really understanding how the person and I could connect. That's why I believe it's important for women to adopt a style of networking that is relational and mutually beneficial to all parties involved. I call this **Net-Connecting**. Net-connecting takes networking a little deeper by planting roots and nurturing the growth of a meaningful relationship between two parties.

I attribute my success in amassing important connections with influencers in women's empowerment and entrepreneurship to gaining a level of mastery with cultivating relationships. It is in fact a simple yet important concept. My success has derived from a dedicated investment of time and energy to support women with their goals, utilizing my skills to help others, offer recommendations and refer women to others if I'm unable to help them. These actions have made the difference for building my valuable network. Now I'm honored to share my secret sauce with you.

My prayer is that this book and the accompanying planner aid you in discovering your genuine and authentic self as well as the best ways to express yourself and build your network.

May God continue to bless you on your journey as you learn to share your greatest asset: YOU!

Eleshia V. Cash
Founder & CEO
Jackson HR & Administrative Services

We are Empowered By What We Learn and Who We are Connected to

In order for an empowered woman to network, she must first understand that a woman is a powerful gift from God to the world. She can walk in her power into any room to be innovative, sensitive, intelligent, strong, compassionate and multi-talented because God has a wonderful plan for her life. It starts with confidence.

Secondly, an empowered woman networks with the understanding that she is walking outside of her comfort zone, moving from comfort to courageous, which is a requirement to experience new things.

Lastly, an empowered woman networks with the intentionality of creating her own network and connections that will propel her to reach her goals. She uses the power of **net-connecting** for this purpose.

"A woman is a powerful gift from God to the world."

How to Use This Book & Planner

*T*he Little Red Networking Book (Women's Empowerment 2nd Edition) & Strategy Planner offers a one-of-a-kind blend of tips and tools to assist women with building a strong network of connections. The book can be used as a standalone reference guide while the strategy planner guides you through planning your networking events, goals and even building your network.

The Strategy Planner includes:
- Inspirational and encouraging messages
- Tracking and accountability sections
- Helpful "insider tips"
- Planning and goal setting sections
- Idea Spot to jot down ideas during moments of inspiration
- Much, much more.

As you use the planner, you will come to consider it a one-stop quick reference guide to all things that involve network building. You may wonder how you've ever attended networking events without considering the preparation activities you will learn about within.

You will have the opportunity to summarize the events you attend, the contacts you make at each event and understand the value you bring to your connections. You can keep track of events that you loved as well as events you were not as impressed with, along with areas to capture notes to refer back to when needed.

Section 1

Build Your Power Squad

Walk By Faith

Build Your Power Squad

*O*utside of God opening doors for me, an important part of my success has been (and still is) my Power Squad. You may be asking, "what is a Power Squad and how do I build one?"

If you have a dream, a goal, or something important that you are trying to accomplish such as starting a business or moving up in your career, you have to establish a network. I like to call this network your **Power Squad.** Your Power Squad helps you accomplish your goals and is what helps you go from Point A to Point B. God's greatest investment is people, and we can't do anything without others. Networking (which I like to call 'Net-connecting') is such a pivotal skill that every person should learn how to do and do well.

Building great relationships opens doors so you can meet other amazing people. Have you ever heard the saying "Iron sharpens iron?" As it relates to net-connecting, this means we are all sharpened by opportunities to rub shoulders with others. In other words, you get to help others with what they need and in turn build skills to enhance yourself as well.

In this chapter, you'll learn about the two different types of networks you should be building simultaneously to determine who will be in your Power Squad.

Building Your Internal & Your External Networks

Women who are just learning about net-connecting must understand the importance of having not just one, but two types of networks: an internal one and an external one. I've found that women who have been working for several years and have existing networks often don't know this.

To illustrate this concept in a way that all women can relate to, I created what I call the **"Open-Toe Shoe/Closed-Toe Shoe Strategy to Building Your Power Squad."**

Build Your Power Squad
Continued

Your Internal Network or "Wearing Your Closed Toe Shoes"

Internal networks are networks that include people we see every day and spend a great deal of time with, like those people at our jobs. It's a fact that African-American women are especially guilty of missing out on relationship-building opportunities because we are so focused on doing the work from 9-to-5 and have no other interactions with co-workers outside of the job. If you truly want to grow your network and ultimately build your Power Squad, it's imperative that you make time for participating in activities with co-workers outside of work hours because this may be the only opportunity for people to connect with you on another level. Others get to see a side of your personality they've never experienced before and find out more about what you like to do in your spare time. They get to "humanize" the person behind the work. Meet up with a co-worker for coffee after work. Have a lunch date. Find out where they are going on their next vacation. Learn more about the other person's family.

You begin to build invested relationships where people feel like they know you, which inevitably can lead to learning "inside" knowledge about what's going on in the workplace. I'm referring to knowledge about promotions, retirements & resignations or learning about a new opportunity that may be opening up before it's announced.

Build Your Power Squad
Continued

Your External Network or "Wearing Your Open Toe Shoes"

Your external network is made up of people outside of your internal network. Where do you start? Start with a list. Really think about who can help you achieve my goals? You can start at the most basic level such as your classmates from high school graduation. That's a network. What are some things you have in common with them? My high school graduating class had over 400 people. There has to be SOMEONE out of these 400 classmates that I have something in common with, right? Ask yourself "Who can help me with moving to the next level?" Is there someone on my job that can help me? Also, it doesn't necessarily have to be someone that you "like." "That lady doesn't really speak to me. She doesn't wave, she doesn't pay me any attention." Put those feelings aside and focus on who can help you get to the next level.

When you graduate from college, keep up with your classmates. Exchange phone numbers, email addresses, connect on Linkedin and engage other social media networks. This could be the key to future internships, jobs, promotions, etc. I can remember this happening to me when I graduated from college. I had a friend named Erica and we were classmates. I reached out to her to let her know that I needed a job and she helped me get a position, just based on her relationship with me. That's often just how easy it can be once you've established and nurtured your network. We have a section dedicated to learning how to nurture your network in this book. It's very important.

Sometimes I refer to what's called an automatic network, and that's one you don't really have to build yourself because your association with an organization helps build it for you. For example, if you graduated from college, you are apart of an alumni association. That's an automatic network you didn't have to build.

Another example of an automatic network is the professional social network called Linkedin. You can search for people based on commonalities you have and Linkedin's algorithm will make the associations or "connections" for you. How easy is that?

Build Your Power Squad
Continued

The algorithm will show you profiles of people "you may know" based on characteristics in your profie, such as employer, college, groups, etc. Use the power of Linkedin to help you find your network online. You can make finding people to network with even more specific according to your career or business specialty, gender and/or ethnic background.

I would always suggest becoming part of a network with the built-in benefit of helping you grow your skillset. For example, if you have a business, join a chamber. They are designed to help you with networking and expanding your skillset. Another example of an automatic network is when you join a professional organization in your industry. For example, if you are an engineer, join a professional association that caters to engineers. You all obviously share a common interest and can share and exchange resources and even job referrals. Get to know the people in the organization and this can be the basis of establishing your network. If you don't have any friends or know anyone, make sure to join an organization. It's a great strategy.

People in your external network show up in other areas of your life like your neighbor, your hairstylist, someone you know at the grocery store, etc.,; pretty much anyone you know outside of work. Your external network includes members of professional, leisure and religious organizations you are a part of (or you need to become a part of). These members can help you navigate your career and business.

Also, remember that the act of networking is not just about getting something from someone else. How can you help others? In the next chapter, you will have an opportunity to figure this out and create a strategy for executing your plan to build a power squad that will continue to bring power to your future career, business and personal endeavors.

Section 2

Develop Your Net-Connecting Strategy

Be still
AND
KNOW
THAT
I am
GOD.
PSALMS 46:10

Develop Your Net-Connecting Strategy

{ **net-connecting** *pron. [net-Kon-NEC-ting]*
noun & (action) verb

"The perfect marriage between networking and building a genuine connection to grow meaningful relationships. }

*I*t's important to be strategic when net-connecting. Possessing an entrepreneurial mindset is critical for achieving your business and career goals. Net-connecting allows visibility to help you progress in your career and business pursuits. Use networking events as a strategy for net-connecting.

Your Personal Brand

It used to be that personal branding was a concept that was only used in connection with celebrities. Now, the concept of personal branding has extended to non-celebrity career-related and business-related pursuits. In fact, it's the norm. A personal brand allows professionals to differentiate themselves from mediocrity. What is a brand? Branding is more than a logo; it is the representation of the reputation that you want people to believe about you and what you offer.

In some cases, branding has been the deciding factor in landing a deal or promotion. The best part of a personal brand is that you have total control over it. It is driven by what you present and how you deliver. For women to develop their brands, it's important to engage in projects, opportunities and initiatives that stretch and strengthen you to progress to the woman you want to become in the near future.

Did you grow up hearing the phrase that girls should be seen and not heard? We are living in a different time now that girls have to be seen and heard if they want to be successful. Part of building your personal brand involves more visibility for yourself and what you do, being seen AND heard. Network like you are your brand at all times.   People need consistency and a level of passion they can relate to.

Develop Your Net-Connecting Strategy
Continued

In your career or business, you represent your brand. Whether a personal brand or a business brand, the way you express the brand in the marketplace is important.

In a business situation, the work you do and the level of engagement with decision makers brings visibility. People will become more familiar with your brand and which will help you open doors for bigger and better opportunities. If people don't know who you are and what you can offer, then they won't choose you when the time arises. Being visible is about being engaged and connected to your market. You can have the best product or service, but without proper visibility it will go unnoticed. Being visible should be made a top priority for success. Use networking events as a strategy to help advertise your brand, in addition to social media and client referrals.

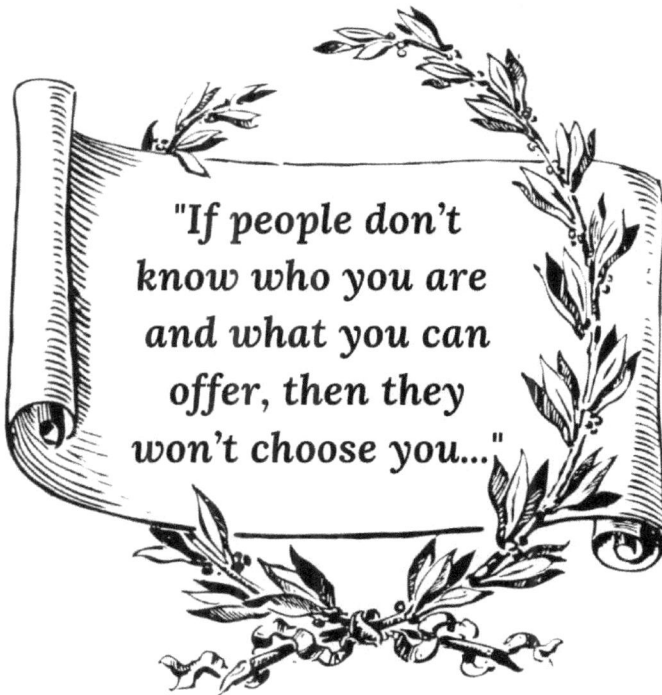

"If people don't know who you are and what you can offer, then they won't choose you..."

Develop Your Net-Connecting Strategy
Continued

Net-connecting affords you the opportunity to gain immediate, direct business from the contacts you make, however you must ensure you are prepared to make the right moves.

The right moves in this case refer to your Power Pitch and your Power Move. In the following paragraphs, you will find more information about each of these concepts.

Developing Your Power Pitch

First off, your power pitch is not synonymous with your elevator pitch. Your power pitch is a one-liner that clearly communicates how valuable you will be as a connection. You speak in terms of how you can help instead of what you actually do.

To demonstrate, review the following examples of someone introducing themselves below. Who would you want to connect with?

Netconnector A	Netconnector B
"I'm a networking consultant."	"I can help you get more partnerships, build your network and referrals and maximize the exposure for your company to gain more revenue."

More Preparation Tips

The next page provides additional tips on preparing your net-connecting strategy.

Develop Your Net-Connecting Strategy
Continued

Tips for Preparation

1

Research the events you are interested in attending. See who will be presenting and the type of audience you will be engaging with.

2

Choose events that will attract like-minded women, experts, or influencers that can enhance your network.

3

Know Your Why. Why this event? Does it put you in the room with other powerful women or influencers that could generate career leads or expand your business?

4

Think ahead. How will you approach the people you wish to meet? It will be wise to do a little research about them prior to attending the event.

5

Identify how you can help others by assessing your own value as a network resource. Women articulate their value to others by looking at the **K**nowledge, **S**kills and **A**bilities (**KSAs**) they possess that can be used to make someone's situation better. Think about your best attributes that are often desired by people in your business or career. Those are the values you can bring to a network. As a resourceful connector, always think about who you have in your network that can assist someone when you are not in the position to do so.

6

Know what your career or business needs help with. The relationships you build should always be mutually beneficial for you and for the other person.

Develop Your Net-Connecting Strategy
Continued

What You Should Do During the Event

During the networking event, you should be collecting important information to ensure that you are able to effectively execute your *POWER MOVE* (more on this a little later).

Here are a few things you should do during the event:

Step One: Collect Contact Information
This is normally done with physical or electronic business cards. Not everyone carries or has business cards, so have your smart phone ready to collect information.

- Use your networking planner to jot down notes. about the people you meet.
- Indicate a special note about each person you meet to include in your follow up email. Write each person's name down to send a message to him/her after the event.
- Create a contact coding system. I will share what I've developed for myself when I talk about the **Power Move**, in the next section.

Step Two: Find the Person on Linkedin
Connect with people you meet on LinkedIn while you are still at the event if possible! Let them know that you've sent a Linkedin request. This is a good way to find out if they are active on this network and if so, it's a good way to communicate with them later.

- Send a personalized note thanking them for accepting your request and reminding the contact of where you met.
- Make sure to also provide your best contact phone number and email.
- This is also a great time to request a phone call to chat or set up a time to meet over coffee.

Develop Your Net-Connecting Strategy
Continued

Step 3: Know How to "Work the Room"

Remember... when you are net-connecting, you want to connect, not just network. This requires a genuine interest in the people in the room.

There is an art to "working a room" and your net-connecting strategies will be your best allies. Working the room requires a confident mindset and strong belief that you're going to an event to have a good time, meet some new people, and make some great connections. Positive energy must enter the room with you.

Make sure you're in a socializing mood. Approach people with the intention of net-connecting with them. When speaking to someone, it is better to be sociable first before launching immediately into business matters. You may want to start by asking one of the following questions:

"Is this your first time attending this event?"

"What other clubs or organizations are you apart of?"

What brought you here today?"

"What are some of the challenges you face in your business or industry?"

"I am apart of XYZ organization, how can I help you with your mission, cause, or business?"

These are great conversation starters that can eventually lead to a potential connection.

Develop Your Net-Connecting Strategy
Continued

The POWER MOVE After the Event

Have you heard the expression "the money is in the follow-up?" The same concept applies to net-connecting. After you've attended a networking event, what you do afterwards can make the difference between building a powerful connection or not. The **Power Move** requires you to *"Work the Net and Work the Connections"*. Make sure this happens within the following 24-48 hours because this is when the real work begins.

As previously mentioned, I developed a special coding system that I use in my networking planner and even to write on the back of business cards I receive during networking events. I've found that doing so helps me to more effectively apply the Power Move afterwards.

My coding system consists of a letter or symbol that I assign to each contact based on the conversation I've had with each one.

> ## My Networking Coding System:
> ## Letter "X", an asterisk (*) or Letter "C"
> (Feel free to use this one or create your own.)

The letter "X" means that the contact receives a generic "it was nice meeting you" email. The "nice meeting you" email is normally an indication that there was not a direct connection, but that it was nice to meet the person. I also share a little about my business or service just in case the person may know someone that could benefit from meeting me.

An asterisk (*) means that the contact will receive an email that says "I would like to add you to my network." This networking email is normally an indication that I would like to add this contact to my network on a long-term basis. Additionally, there is high potential for me to directly support the contact or to refer others to this contact.

Develop Your Net-Connecting Strategy
Continued

The letter "C " means that the contact that will receive an emai that says " I would like to connect with you." If I made a connection I would like to nurture this relationship. This email provides specific information we spoke about when we met, information about a similar event to attend, as well as an invitation for a coffee chat or a scheduled phone meeting.

Remember that the follow up should be completed within 48-hours.

The "POWER WIN" Strategy

The **Power Win Strategy** is key to ensuring a win-win for everyone involved. This strategy addresses reciprocity, authenticity, and shared values because it's very important that both you and the other party equally gain when net-connecting.

To enact this strategy, both parties will meet to have a conversation that would address the other's needs and create an action plan to resolve those needs.   Before you meet, think of and write out three issues or problems that each of you want to address in your business, career or ministry. When you come together, the two (or more) of you will discuss ways to resolve the issue and how each of you can benefit.

When you utilize this Power Win Strategy, you apply another net-connecting power concept called the ***"Support, Promote, or Refer"*** concept. In this strategy, each person is setup to win and gain success from the other partner supporting her efforts, promoting her efforts and referring her brand, skills and/or business to others. Each person equally gains to ensure that no one feels slighted, cheated or used in the process.

To expand further on the "Refer" portion of this concept, understand that one of the the fastest ways to grow your own network is to introduce two people who can benefit from each other.

Develop Your Net-Connecting Strategy
Continued

I've found that women sometimes tend to refrain from sharing their connections with others they meet because it's not clear how they would personally benefit from the referrals they share. News flash! You will not always gain something directly from a networking relationship.

As the connector, you are building a stronger network with multiple people. It's been said that your "network is your net worth." Doing so adds value to your net worth in this case as well as your relationship building prowess. Additionally, it has the positive effect of increasing your influence in the process.

Now that you have your "Power" tools, you can position yourself for growth and success largely through net-connecting.

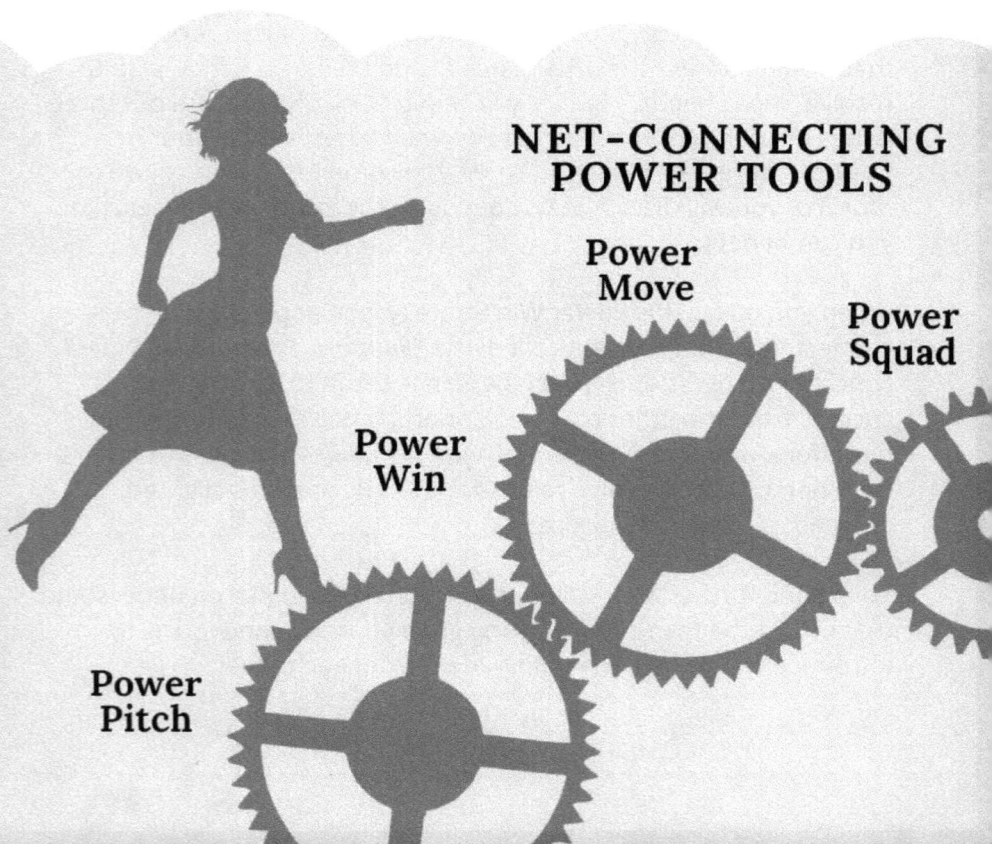

NET-CONNECTING POWER TOOLS

Power Move

Power Squad

Power Win

Power Pitch

Section 3
Establish Collaborative Partnerships

LET YOUR LIGHT SHINE

Establish Collaborative Partnerships

*I*f women thought about partnerships and collaboration the way we think about shoes, we would excel in our businesses, ministries and non-profits. Women work so much better together and we can achieve more in collaboration if we consider the following concepts:

1. Heels on Common Ground

The single most important factor in any partnership is that you and your partner are on the same page. Finding a partner that believes in what you believe in and also upholds the same standards will be critical at every decision point in your business journey.

2. Wear the Same Sized Shoes

Purpose speaks to why we are dong what we do. Where are you going? Collaborators must see that the shoes are a good fit, regarding the direction of the business, and the impact those shoes will make on t he journey to success.

3. Shop for Shoes in Different Places

The best partnerships include women who have different skills. You don't need duplicates in a partnership.

We don't need to show up to a meeting with the same pair of shoes on. Having great minds that think alike in the partnership will not necessarily render the best results in this case.

For example, one person may be the visionary and the other one is the project manager. Your partner should fill the gaps and contribute to the strengths needed for a successful partnership, not simply add the same skillset you already bring from your KSAs.

Establish Collaborative Partnerships
Continued

"If women thought about partnerships and collaboration the way we think about shoes, we would excel in our businesses, ministries and non-profits."

Women work better together!

Women could achieve more in collaboration if we consider the following concepts:

1 Heels on Common Ground

2 Wear the Same Sized Shoes

3 Shop for Shoes in Different Places

Section 4

Re-Evaluate Your Current Network

FOR I
know
THE PLANS
I HAVE FOR
you...
JEREMIAH 29:11

Re-Evaluate Your Current Network

*I*n order to build your network, you have to start somewhere. It's best to start with what you already have. You may be surprised to find that you have a number of people already within your current circles that are willing, ready and/or able to support you in your endeavors. They are just waiting to hear from you. That's why it's SO important to nurture the people in your network and deepen the connections with them.

I find that seasoned professionals often have challenges with understanding the value of their networks, especially in this era of social media. We often miss out on leveraging our networks properly. When we get stuck in our careers and businesses, we should take inventory of our networks to see who can help us move forward. This is surely a necessary and worthwhile exercise.

Once you've completed this re-evauation of your network, consider the following tips to refresh your network:

- Join a small networking group
- Attend a Meetup function and/or community organization event
- Participate in an outreach ministry.
- Look at organizations within your church or workplace.
- Seek out external groups that support and highlight your hobbies or other special interests you may have.
- Review your social media activity to see if there are associated groups that may be of interest.

In addition to the above tips, professional associations, alumni groups, clubs, and personal interest communities are often the source of establishing real connections and building networks for career advancement and business growth.

Re-Evaluate Your Current Network

Continued

Start with the organizations you are already apart of. People have to know who you are, what you do, what you believe in, and how they can help you in order to best serve you and vice versa.

In the Strategy Planner, you will have an opportunity to explore and reflect upon people within your existing network.

It's not about the size of your network, but the quality of connections within it. If you are engaged with the people you are connected to, than your net work has more value. Quality connections are worth a hundred times more in value than in quantity.

"People have to know who you are, what you do, what you believe in, and how they can help you in order to best serve you and vice versa."

Section 5

Nurture Your Network

The
CHEERFUL
heart
» HAS A «
CONTINUAL
feast
PROVERBS 15:15

Nurture Your Network

*W*e've all had people who have contacted us out of the blue after years of never touching base. When that happens, it's difficult to support them because they haven't put any effort into sustaining the relationship. Nurturing relationships is one important key to building a strong network. Below are a few tips on how to nurture your network.

Send physical greeting card or handwritten note (postcards count too)

Send a quick text message, phone call or email

Contact via social media platforms on which you've connected with your network

Reach out for a social meeting (i.e. Coffee Chat or Meetups)

It's imperative to "touch" your contacts at least three to four times a year. After you choose the right people to network with, remember to stay in contact with them.

If you are involved in the right kinds of networking groups and activities your contacts are expecting you to ask them for help. If you offer your support, your networking partners will certainly want to return the favor.

Grateful **THANKFUL** *Blessed*

Nurture Your Network
Continued

Transform Social Media Networks into Real-Life Contacts

Although the social networks can be very beneficial, entrepreneurs should not totally rely on them as primary vehicles for communication and networking. You still have to "get out there", shake a few hands and have a conversation over a glass of wine or a cup of coffee. Social networks open the door to opportunities to meet new people, but people are still very relational when it comes to doing business.

Follow people on social media who inspire you to grow and who are difference makers in the industry you want to get into or are already apart of. Join their groups.

In those groups, make connections that lead to:

In-Person Meetings

to

Video Chats

to

Phone Calls

to

Accountability Partners

Social media allows you or your organization to engage current and potential supporters in an organic, genuine way that is noninvasive, yet socially consistent. Social media is especially helpful when it comes to finding out about current events, volunteering opportunities, etc. Joining empowered, exclusive groups on social media platforms allows you to make professional connections and stay abreast of current knowledge and trends within your industry.

Nurture Your Network
Continued

Organize a System to Keep Track of Existing Relationships

I encourage you to invest in a CRM (Customer Relationship Management) system to keep track of existing relationships and leads. You can go from a very basic setup to one with all the bells and whistles, however the objective is to move contacts from your phone to a visual database that will assist you with increasing profitability for your business and to gain opportunities for career advancement.

One of my favorite start-up systems to use is Mailchimp.   Mailchimp is a powerful marketing automation platform that's easy to use and works really well. As your network expands, you will find the need to begin managing this expansion. Starting small will prove beneficial as your network grows.

Nurture the Relationship BEFORE You Need It

Sometimes when it's time to "ask" your network for help, you may not be sure how to do it. Remember, networking is about building connections and relationships. If you've been nurturing the relationship from the start, then the "ask" is much less awkward. Make sure to use the "**Power Win**" strategy to build your network as it makes your "ask" a natural part of the net-connecting relationship. Keep the following in mind:

> **Be reasonable.**
> *Is your ask in proportion to the relationship that you've developed?*
>
> **Be simple.**
> *Don't ask for too many things at one time.*
>
> **Be Precise.**
> *Take some time to plan your message.*
> *Avoid being vague or ambiguous.*

Section *6*

Tips for Introverts

BLESSED IS She WHO BELIEVED

Tips for Introverts

I can certainly relate to being an introvert. When my husband decided that he wanted to start a ministry, I was not in the mental space to be a Pastor's wife. I would have to now be in the public eye, kiss babies and shake hands with people in the congregation and when we went to travel to other churches and conferences. This may have been the defining moment to help me break out of my shell when it came to networking. I do realize that this is not everyone's situation and I have compassion for those that identify as an introvert. It is not an easy road to networking, but it is definitely one that you can overcome and get better at.

What I found helpful for "dipping your toe" in the networking pool is to use social media as a way to get acclimated to introducing yourself to others without having to do it in person, at least initially. I say that because you can still "hide behind the keyboard" so to speak and create and/or participate in conversations by posting comments, writing articles and sharing your voice on topics you are passionate about. When you are ready, you can go to the next step of posting pictures and creating videos so that others can see the face behind the voice. Attending live zoom sessions and conferences can be the next step forward and then eventually attending live conferences if you don't already do so will be a good progression to getting more comfortable with networking. Truly leverage social media as way to practice building your networking skills. Doing so greatly increased my confidence in interacting with others, speaking with them away from social media and then using those opportunities to build my power network.

For those of you that still struggle with networking and perhaps even social anxiety, and think social media may be too much of a leap, I have two words of advice for you; Start & Embrace.

#1 Start.
You have to start somewhere and I recommend starting with social media. Create a professional profile on Linkedin. Join a special interest group on a social media platform, then begin liking, commenting, and eventually sharing your own post.

Tips for Introverts
Continued

#2 Embrace.

Embrace the moment. Don't let a momentary uncomfortable experience hold you back from success! We are empowered by what we learn and what we are exposed to. These moments provide exposure and an opportunity to practice what we learn, so that an empowered transformation will take place when we begin to master the skill.

"...She can walk in her power into any room to be innovative, sensitive, intelligent, strong, compassionate and multi-talented because God has a wonderful plan for her life. It starts with confidence."

Section 7

Know When to "Level Up" Your Network

God IS IN control AND His Timing IS PERFECT

Know When to "Level" Up Your Network

*H*ow do you know when it's time to expand your network? Well, your network should be consistently growing. It is hard to grow and advance to bigger and better accomplishments when you are around the same people all the time.   At some point you will need to "Level Up" which begins with changing your environment and being around people who inspire you to dream bigger and contribute more which adds to your value, growth and development.

WE RISE BY *lifting* OTHERS

If your current connections don't inspire you to do more and be more, than this is an indication that you must push past your comfort zone and explore new territories. We are empowered by what we learn and what we are exposed to.   When you are exposed to the right people within your networks, you place yourself in the pathway of opportunity.

Remember, the **"Power Win"** strategy. Everyone involved should win. It's very important that you and the other party both equally gain when net-connecting. If you don't see where you are winning in the relationship, than this could be a sign that it's time to "level up" your network.

My Notes

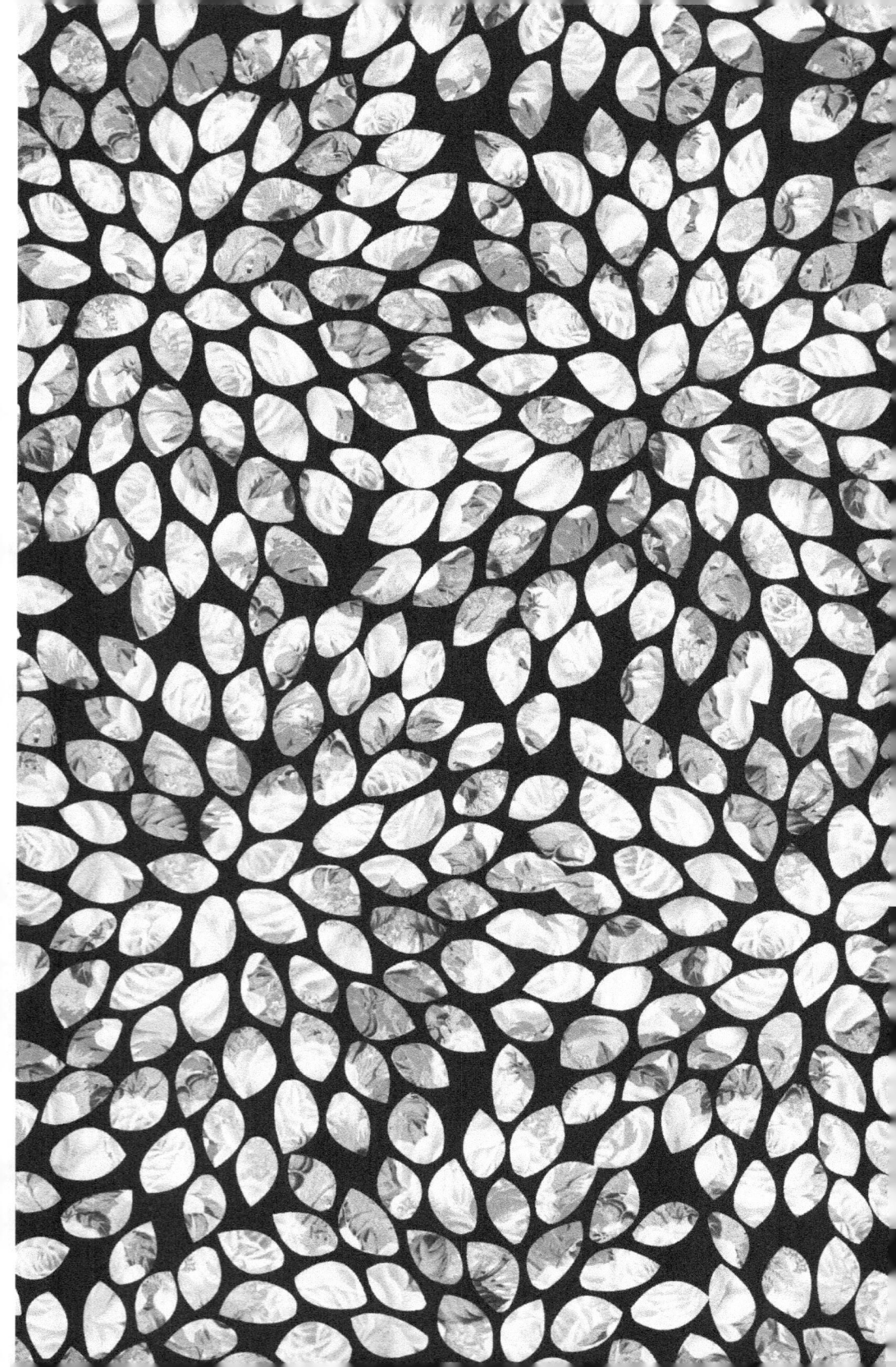

Contents of the Strategy Planner

*An undated planner allows you to conveniently pick up where you left off at any point in the year without wasting precious pages that you might waste using a dated planner. You can write in a guiding quote or scripture for the month as well as a theme to help guide the types of events and activities you are seeking to find and engage in.

Contents of the Strategy Planner

Part 6: Past Event Summaries Page 121

This section allows you to capture a high level summary of events you've
attended. It is meant to act as a quick reference guide to keep track
of past events with a few details about the event including whether
or not you'd attend again.

Part 7: My POWER MOVES Page 137

This is the section where you will keep up with your POWER MOVES
as the book describes. There are specific details you can capture for
each contact that will be helpful as you build your network.

Part 8: My Notes Page 159

This section is available for you to jot down quick ideas and thoughts
as you attend and participate in net-connecting events and activities.

Part 1

Identify My KSAs

In Section 2: Developing Your Net-Connecting Strategy it talks about getting prepared for net-connecting. Tip #5 recommended that you should **"identify how you can help others by assessing your own value as a network resource" using your Knowledge, Skills and Abilities,** in other words, **your KSAs**.

Use the following pages to identify your unique KSAs.

Identify My KSAs

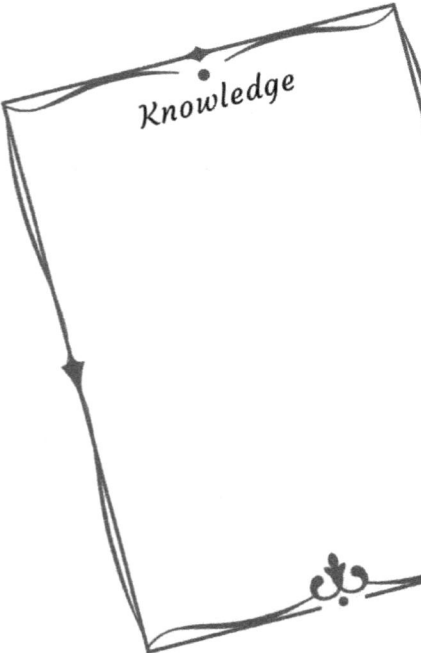

Knowledge

Knowledge

Knowledge

Identify My KSAs

Skills

Skills

Skills

Identify My KSAs

Abilities

Abilities

Abilities

Part 2
Craft My Power Pitch

Use this section to craft your Power Pitch as described in Section 2 of the book.

Craft My Power Pitch

*A*s explained in Section 2 of the book, your power pitch is a one-liner that clearly communicates how valuable you will be as a connection. You speak in terms of how you can help instead of what you actually do.

Use the space below to transform your KSAs into a powerful description of how you can help someone in your network when called upon.

My KSAs

Knowledge

_____
_____
_____
_____
_____
_____
_____
_____
_____
_____
_____
_____
_____

Skills

_____
_____
_____
_____
_____
_____
_____
_____
_____
_____
_____
_____

Abilities

_____
_____
_____
_____
_____

MY POWER PITCH

_____
_____
_____
_____
_____

Part 3
Re-Evaluate My Current Network

This section provides space to write down members of your current network under easily identifiable categories.

Re-Evaluate My Current Network

*I*n this section, you will create several lists of contacts within your existing network. It is recommended to first create the lists, then go back and assign a "network code" in the space provided within the "code" column. If you didn't create your own coding system, feel free to use the one I created as explained below. An example of how to apply a code is provided on the following page.

> ## My Networking Coding System:
> ## "X", (*) or "C"

The letter **"X"** means that the contact receives a generic "it was nice meeting you" email. The "nice meeting you" email is normally an indication that there was not a direct connection, but that it was nice meeting the person. I also share a little about my business or service just in case the person may know someone that could benefit from meeting me.

An asterisk **(*)** means that the contact will receive an email that says "I would like to add you to my network." This networking email is normally an indication that I would like to add this contact to my network on a long-term basis. Additionally, there is a possibility for me to support something the contact is doing or to refer someone to this contact.

The letter **"C "** means that the contact that will receive an email that says "I would like to connect with you." If I made a connection I would like to nurture this relationship. This networking email is normally an indication that I would like to add this contact to my network on a long-term basis. Additionally, there is high potential for me to directly support the contact or to refer others to this contact.

Re-Evaluate My Current Network

*Example of Using the Coding System on the following pages.**

Colleagues from College & Graduate School

(Sororities, Fraternities, Clubs, Teams, Alumni Networks, Professors, etc.) In the 1st column list the activity/group, and in the 2nd column list the contact's name.

UNC Charlotte	C	Shannon Wesley
FAMU	*	Karen Gordon

*The Family & Friends page is different than the other pages. Please write in the code under the columns provided.

Re-Evaluate My Current Network

Use the following pages to list the people that currently exist in your network under each appropriate category listed. **Make a Power Move!**

Family & Close Friends

Make a list of family and friends that can add value to your pursuits. You never know what connections they have, so make sure you think it through.

	Code		Code

Re-Evaluate My Current Network

Use the following pages to list the people that currently exist in your network under each appropriate category listed. **Make a Power Move!**

Family & Close Friends

Make a list of family and friends that can add value to your pursuits. You never know what connections they have, so make sure you think it through.

	Code		Code

Re-Evaluate My Current Network

Use the following pages to list the people that currently exist in your network under each appropriate category listed. ***Make a Power Move!***

Colleagues from College & Graduate School

(Sororities, Fraternities, Clubs, Teams, Alumni Networks, Professors, etc.) In the 1st column list the activity/group, and in the 2nd column list the contact's name.

	Code	

Re-Evaluate My Current Network

Use the following pages to list the people that currently exist in your network under each appropriate category listed. **_Make a Power Move!_**

Colleagues from College & Graduate School

(Sororities, Fraternities, Clubs, Teams, Alumni Networks, Professors, etc.) In the 1st column list the activity/group, and in the 2nd column list the contact's name.

	Code	

Re-Evaluate My Current Network

Use the following pages to list the people that currently exist in your network under each appropriate category listed. ***Make a Power Move!***

Colleagues from Past/Current Education & Training

(High School, Conferences, Workshops, Vendor training, etc. In the 1st column, list the place/training and in the 2nd column, list the contact's name)

	Code	

Re-Evaluate My Current Network

Use the following pages to list the people that currently exist in your network under each appropriate category listed. **Make a Power Move!**

Colleagues from Past/Current Education & Training

(High School, Conferences, Workshops, Vendor training, etc. In the 1st column, list the place/training and in the 2nd column, list the contact's name)

	Code	

Re-Evaluate My Current Network

Use the following pages to list the people that currently exist in your network under each appropriate category listed. *Make a Power Move!*

Colleagues from Faith-Based Community
(Churches, Synagogues, Mosques, etc.) Current and past affiliations.

	Code	

Re-Evaluate My Current Network

Use the following pages to list the people that currently exist in your network under each appropriate category listed. **Make a Power Move!**

Colleagues from Faith-Based Community
(Churches, Synagogues, Mosques, etc.) Current and past affiliations.

	Code	

Re-Evaluate My Current Network

Use the following pages to list the people that currently exist in your network under each appropriate category listed. **Make a Power Move!**

List of My Memberships, Clubs & Activities

List all memberships, clubs and activities you are actively engaged in or were in the past In the 1st column, list current ones and in the 2nd column list those from the past. Use the guiding information on the next page to create your list.

	Code	

Re-Evaluate My Current Network

Use the following pages to list the people that currently exist in your network under each appropriate category listed. **Make a Power Move!**

Colleagues from Memberships & Clubs
(Greek-Letter Organizations, Professional Development,
Employment-Related Activities, Social Clubs, Hobbies, etc..)

	Code	

Re-Evaluate My Current Network

Use the following pages to list the people that currently exist in your network under each appropriate category listed. **Make a Power Move!**

Colleagues from Memberships & Clubs
(Greek-Letter Organizations, Professional Development, Employment-Related Activities, Social Clubs, Hobbies, etc..)

	Code	

Re-Evaluate My Current Network

Use the following pages to list the people that currently exist in your network under each appropriate category listed. **Make a Power Move!**

Colleagues from Leisure Activities

(Hobbies, interests, Passions, Past-times, Social Media Groups, etc.) List the activity in the 1st column and the contact's name in the 2nd column.

	Code	

Re-Evaluate My Current Network

Use the following pages to list the people that currently exist in your network under each appropriate category listed. *Make a Power Move!*

Colleagues from Leisure Activities

(Hobbies, interests, Passions, Past-times, Social Media Groups, etc.) List the activity in the 1st column and the contact's name in the 2nd column.

	Code	

Re-Evaluate My Current Network

Use the following pages to list the people that currently exist in your network under each appropriate category listed. ***Make a Power Move!***

Colleagues from Daily Routines

(Grocery Store, Barber/Beauty Salon, Nail Salon, Cleaners, Restaurants, Fitness Activities, Caregivers, Health Occupations, Cleaners, Financial Services, etc.) List the service in 1st column and the contact's name in the 2nd column.

	Code	

Re-Evaluate My Current Network

Use the following pages to list the people that currently exist in your network under each appropriate category listed. **Make a Power Move!**

Colleagues from Daily Routines

(Grocery Store, Barber/Beauty Salon, Nail Salon, Cleaners, Restaurants, Fitness Activities, Caregivers, Health Occupations, Cleaners, Financial Services, etc.) List the service in 1st column and the contact's name in the 2nd column.

	Code	

Re-Evaluate My Current Network

Use the following pages to list the people that currently exist in your network under each appropriate category listed. **Make a Power Move!**

Colleagues from Social Media (Part 1)

Make a list of social media platforms you interact with on a frequent basis. In Part 2, you will list different contacts you have/people you follow on them.

	Code	

Re-Evaluate My Current Network

Use the following pages to list the people that currently exist in your network under each appropriate category listed. **Make a Power Move!**

Colleagues from Social Media (Part 2)

List contacts you have, people you follow or that follow you. List the social media platform in the 1st column and the name or handle in the 2nd column.

	Code	

Re-Evaluate My Current Network

Use the following pages to list the people that currently exist in your network under each appropriate category listed. *Make a Power Move!*

Colleagues from Social Media (Part 2)

List contacts you have, people you follow or that follow you. List the social media platform in the 1st column and the name or handle in the 2nd column.

	Code	

Re-Evaluate My Current Network

Use the following pages to list the people that currently exist in your network under each appropriate category listed. *Make a Power Move!*

Colleagues from Current/Past Employers

List the employer's name in the 1st column along with the years you were there and the contact's name in the 2nd column.

	Code	

Re-Evaluate My Current Network

Use the following pages to list the people that currently exist in your network under each appropriate category listed. ***Make a Power Move!***

Colleagues from Current/Past Employers
List the employer's name in the 1st column along with the years you were there and the contact's name in the 2nd column.

	Code	

Re-Evaluate My Current Network

Use the following pages to list the people that currently exist in your network under each appropriate category listed. **Make a Power Move!**

Current Clients and/or Business Partners

List the service you provided or company name in the 1st column and the contact's name in the 2nd column.

	Code	

Re-Evaluate My Current Network

Use the following pages to list the people that currently exist in your network under each appropriate category listed. ***Make a Power Move!***

Current Clients and/or Business Partners
List the service you provided or company name in the 1st column and the contact's name in the 2nd column.

	Code	

Re-Evaluate My Current Network

Use the following pages to list the people that currently exist in your network under each appropriate category listed. *Make a Power Move!*

Past Clients and/or Business Partners

List the service you provided or company name in the 1st column and the contact's name in the 2nd column.

	Code	

Re-Evaluate My Current Network

Use the following pages to list the people that currently exist in your network under each appropriate category listed. **Make a Power Move!**

Past Clients and/or Business Partners

List the service you provided or company name in the 1st column and the contact's name in the 2nd column.

	Code	

Re-Evaluate My Current Network

Use the following pages to list the people that currently exist in your network under each appropriate category listed. *Make a Power Move!*

Colleagues from Volunteer Activities
List the organization/non-profit in the 1st column and the contact's name in the 2nd column.

	Code	

Re-Evaluate My Current Network

Use the following pages to list the people that currently exist in your network under each appropriate category listed. *Make a Power Move!*

Colleagues from Volunteer Activities

List the organization/non-profit in the 1st column and the contact's name in the 2nd column.

	Code	

Re-Evaluate My Current Network

Use the following pages to list the people that currently exist in your network under each appropriate category listed. *Make a Power Move!*

Other Contacts

	Code	

Re-Evaluate My Current Network

Use the following pages to list the people that currently exist in your network under each appropriate category listed. *Make a Power Move!*

Other Contacts

	Code	

Part 4
Planning My Net-Connecting Activities

In this section, you will identify your overall goals for the year to guide your net-connecting event and activity planning.

Annual Net-Connecting Goals

✔ **My Goals for the Year** (*Check off & celebrate when achieved*)

Key Contacts I'd Like to Make

Key Professions to Collaborate With For Growth

Annual Net-Connecting Goals

Thoughts about My Net-Connecting Strategy to Achieve My Goals

Guiding Quotes/Scriptures

Annual Net-Connecting Goals

Events Recommended From Last Year

In-Person Organizations/Groups I Want to Check Out

Social Media Organizations/Groups I May Join

Annual Net-Connecting Goals

How I measure goal achievement? In other words, how will I know that my goals have been achieved?

Rewards for Achieving Goals

Other Notes for this Section

Events to Attend This Year

DAY		DATE	EVENT	TIME
Mo Tu We Th Fr Sa Su		___/___/___		___:___
Mo Tu We Th Fr Sa Su		___/___/___		___:___
Mo Tu We Th Fr Sa Su		___/___/___		___:___
Mo Tu We Th Fr Sa Su		___/___/___		___:___
Mo Tu We Th Fr Sa Su		___/___/___		___:___
Mo Tu We Th Fr Sa Su		___/___/___		___:___
Mo Tu We Th Fr Sa Su		___/___/___		___:___
Mo Tu We Th Fr Sa Su		___/___/___		___:___
Mo Tu We Th Fr Sa Su		___/___/___		___:___
Mo Tu We Th Fr Sa Su		___/___/___		___:___
Mo Tu We Th Fr Sa Su		___/___/___		___:___
Mo Tu We Th Fr Sa Su		___/___/___		___:___
Mo Tu We Th Fr Sa Su		___/___/___		___:___
Mo Tu We Th Fr Sa Su		___/___/___		___:___
Mo Tu We Th Fr Sa Su		___/___/___		___:___
Mo Tu We Th Fr Sa Su		___/___/___		___:___
Mo Tu We Th Fr Sa Su		___/___/___		___:___
Mo Tu We Th Fr Sa Su		___/___/___		___:___

Events to Attend This Year

DAY	DATE	EVENT	TIME
Mo Tu We Th Fr Sa Su	__/__/__		__:__
Mo Tu We Th Fr Sa Su	__/__/__		__:__
Mo Tu We Th Fr Sa Su	__/__/__		__:__
Mo Tu We Th Fr Sa Su	__/__/__		__:__
Mo Tu We Th Fr Sa Su	__/__/__		__:__
Mo Tu We Th Fr Sa Su	__/__/__		__:__
Mo Tu We Th Fr Sa Su	__/__/__		__:__
Mo Tu We Th Fr Sa Su	__/__/__		__:__
Mo Tu We Th Fr Sa Su	__/__/__		__:__
Mo Tu We Th Fr Sa Su	__/__/__		__:__
Mo Tu We Th Fr Sa Su	__/__/__		__:__
Mo Tu We Th Fr Sa Su	__/__/__		__:__
Mo Tu We Th Fr Sa Su	__/__/__		__:__
Mo Tu We Th Fr Sa Su	__/__/__		__:__
Mo Tu We Th Fr Sa Su	__/__/__		__:__
Mo Tu We Th Fr Sa Su	__/__/__		__:__
Mo Tu We Th Fr Sa Su	__/__/__		__:__
Mo Tu We Th Fr Sa Su	__/__/__		__:__
Mo Tu We Th Fr Sa Su	__/__/__		__:__

Events to Attend This Year

DAY	DATE	EVENT	TIME
Mo Tu We Th Fr Sa Su	__/__/__		__:__
Mo Tu We Th Fr Sa Su	__/__/__		__:__
Mo Tu We Th Fr Sa Su	__/__/__		__:__
Mo Tu We Th Fr Sa Su	__/__/__		__:__
Mo Tu We Th Fr Sa Su	__/__/__		__:__
Mo Tu We Th Fr Sa Su	__/__/__		__:__
Mo Tu We Th Fr Sa Su	__/__/__		__:__
Mo Tu We Th Fr Sa Su	__/__/__		__:__
Mo Tu We Th Fr Sa Su	__/__/__		__:__
Mo Tu We Th Fr Sa Su	__/__/__		__:__
Mo Tu We Th Fr Sa Su	__/__/__		__:__
Mo Tu We Th Fr Sa Su	__/__/__		__:__
Mo Tu We Th Fr Sa Su	__/__/__		__:__
Mo Tu We Th Fr Sa Su	__/__/__		__:__
Mo Tu We Th Fr Sa Su	__/__/__		__:__
Mo Tu We Th Fr Sa Su	__/__/__		__:__
Mo Tu We Th Fr Sa Su	__/__/__		__:__
Mo Tu We Th Fr Sa Su	__/__/__		__:__

Events to Attend This Year

DAY	DATE	EVENT	TIME
Mo Tu We Th Fr Sa Su	__/__/__		__:__
Mo Tu We Th Fr Sa Su	__/__/__		__:__
Mo Tu We Th Fr Sa Su	__/__/__		__:__
Mo Tu We Th Fr Sa Su	__/__/__		__:__
Mo Tu We Th Fr Sa Su	__/__/__		__:__
Mo Tu We Th Fr Sa Su	__/__/__		__:__
Mo Tu We Th Fr Sa Su	__/__/__		__:__
Mo Tu We Th Fr Sa Su	__/__/__		__:__
Mo Tu We Th Fr Sa Su	__/__/__		__:__
Mo Tu We Th Fr Sa Su	__/__/__		__:__
Mo Tu We Th Fr Sa Su	__/__/__		__:__
Mo Tu We Th Fr Sa Su	__/__/__		__:__
Mo Tu We Th Fr Sa Su	__/__/__		__:__
Mo Tu We Th Fr Sa Su	__/__/__		__:__
Mo Tu We Th Fr Sa Su	__/__/__		__:__
Mo Tu We Th Fr Sa Su	__/__/__		__:__
Mo Tu We Th Fr Sa Su	__/__/__		__:__
Mo Tu We Th Fr Sa Su	__/__/__		__:__
Mo Tu We Th Fr Sa Su	__/__/__		__:__

Part 5
My Monthly Net-Connecting Calendar & Event Recap

This section provides an undated monthly calendar for a quick glance of highlighted days for which you have designated to perform net-connecting activities such as:

*Making Power Moves
*Attending events
*Meeting contacts, etc.

This section also provides space to highlight costs during the month so that you can keep track of your net-connecting budget and key contacts you've made during the month. You also quickly reference events and activities you liked and didn't like as well as identify goals accomplished and lessons learned.

Monthly Net-Connecting Calendar

Month _____ Year _____

Sunday	Monday	Tuesday	Wednesday	Thursday	Friday	Saturday

Quote/Scripture of the Month

Theme For This Month's Net-Connecting Activities

Monthly Event Summary & Recap

Month _____ Year _____

Total # of Events Attended This Month

Total Spent	Week 1	Week 2	Week 3	Week 4		Total
Planned Monthly Budget	$				=	$
$		Is Total Under Planned Budget?		Is Total Over Planned Budget?		

Key Contacts I Met This Month

Followed Up?

My Favorite Networking Event(s)/Activities This Month & Why

My Least Favorite Networking Event(s)/Activities This Month & Why

Goals Accomplished; Major Tasks Completed

Lessons Learned

Monthly Net-Connecting Calendar

Month _____ Year _____

Sunday	Monday	Tuesday	Wednesday	Thursday	Friday	Saturday

Quote/Scripture of the Month

Theme For This Month's Net-Connecting Activities

Monthly Event Summary & Recap

Month _____ Year _____

Total # of Events Attended This Month

Total Spent	Week 1	Week 2	Week 3	Week 4		Total
Planned Monthly Budget $	$				=	$
		Is Total Under Planned Budget?		Is Total Over Planned Budget?		

Key Contacts I Met This Month   Followed Up?

My Favorite Networking Event(s)/Activities This Month & Why

My Least Favorite Networking Event(s)/Activities This Month & Why

Goals Accomplished; Major Tasks Completed

Lessons Learned

Monthly Net-Connecting Calendar

Month _____ Year _____

Sunday	Monday	Tuesday	Wednesday	Thursday	Friday	Saturday

Quote/Scripture of the Month

Theme For This Month's Net-Connecting Activities

Monthly Event Summary & Recap

Month _____ Year _____

Total # of Events Attended This Month

Total Spent	Week 1	Week 2	Week 3	Week 4		Total
	$				=	$
Planned Monthly Budget $		Is Total Under Planned Budget?		Is Total Over Planned Budget?		

Key Contacts I Met This Month
Followed Up?

My Favorite Networking Event(s)/Activities This Month & Why

My Least Favorite Networking Event(s)/Activities This Month & Why

Goals Accomplished; Major Tasks Completed

Lessons Learned

Monthly Net-Connecting Calendar

Month _____ Year _____

Sunday	Monday	Tuesday	Wednesday	Thursday	Friday	Saturday

Quote/Scripture of the Month

Theme For This Month's Net-Connecting Activities

Monthly Event Summary & Recap

Month _____ Year _____

Total # of Events Attended This Month

Total Spent	Week 1	Week 2	Week 3	Week 4		Total
Planned Monthly Budget $	$				=	$
		Is Total Under Planned Budget?		Is Total Over Planned Budget?		

Key Contacts I Met This Month

Followed
Up?

My Favorite Networking Event(s)/Activities This Month & Why

My Least Favorite Networking Event(s)/Activities This Month & Why

Goals Accomplished; Major Tasks Completed

Lessons Learned

Monthly Net-Connecting Calendar

Month _____ Year _____

Sunday	Monday	Tuesday	Wednesday	Thursday	Friday	Saturday

Quote/Scripture of the Month

Theme For This Month's Net-Connecting Activities

Monthly Event Summary & Recap

Month _____ Year _____

Total # of Events Attended This Month

Total Spent	Week 1	Week 2	Week 3	Week 4		Total
	$				=	$
Planned Monthly Budget $		Is Total Under Planned Budget?		Is Total Over Planned Budget?		

Key Contacts I Met This Month   Followed Up?

My Favorite Networking Event(s)/Activities This Month & Why

My Least Favorite Networking Event(s)/Activities This Month & Why

Goals Accomplished; Major Tasks Completed

Lessons Learned

Monthly Net-Connecting Calendar

Month _____ Year _____

Sunday	Monday	Tuesday	Wednesday	Thursday	Friday	Saturday

Quote/Scripture of the Month

Theme For This Month's Net-Connecting Activities

Monthly Event Summary & Recap

Month _____ Year _____

Total # of Events Attended This Month

Total Spent	Week 1	Week 2	Week 3	Week 4		Total
	$				=	$
Planned Monthly Budget $	Is Total Under Planned Budget?			Is Total Over Planned Budget?		

Key Contacts I Met This Month

Followed Up?

My Favorite Networking Event(s)/Activities This Month & Why

My Least Favorite Networking Event(s)/Activities This Month & Why

Goals Accomplished; Major Tasks Completed

Lessons Learned

Monthly Net-Connecting Calendar

Month _____ Year _____

Sunday	Monday	Tuesday	Wednesday	Thursday	Friday	Saturday

Quote/Scripture of the Month

Theme For This Month's Net-Connecting Activities

Monthly Event Summary & Recap

Month _____ Year _____

Total # of Events Attended This Month

Total Spent	Week 1	Week 2	Week 3	Week 4		Total
	$				=	$
Planned Monthly Budget $		Is Total Under Planned Budget?		Is Total Over Planned Budget?		

Key Contacts I Met This Month   Followed Up?

My Favorite Networking Event(s)/Activities This Month & Why

My Least Favorite Networking Event(s)/Activities This Month & Why

Goals Accomplished; Major Tasks Completed

Lessons Learned

Monthly Net-Connecting Calendar

Month _____ Year _____

Sunday	Monday	Tuesday	Wednesday	Thursday	Friday	Saturday

Quote/Scripture of the Month

Theme For This Month's Net-Connecting Activities

Monthly Event Summary & Recap

Month _____ Year _____

Total # of Events Attended This Month

Total Spent	Week 1	Week 2	Week 3	Week 4		Total
Planned Monthly Budget $	$				=	$
	Is Total Under Planned Budget?			Is Total Over Planned Budget?		

Key Contacts I Met This Month

Followed Up?

My Favorite Networking Event(s)/Activities This Month & Why

My Least Favorite Networking Event(s)/Activities This Month & Why

Goals Accomplished; Major Tasks Completed

Lessons Learned

Monthly Net-Connecting Calendar

Month _____ Year _____

Sunday	Monday	Tuesday	Wednesday	Thursday	Friday	Saturday

Quote/Scripture of the Month

Theme For This Month's Net-Connecting Activities

Monthly Event Summary & Recap

Month _____ Year _____

Total # of Events Attended This Month

Total Spent	Week 1	Week 2	Week 3	Week 4		Total
	$				=	$
Planned Monthly Budget $		Is Total Under Planned Budget?		Is Total Over Planned Budget?		

Key Contacts I Met This Month   Followed Up?

My Favorite Networking Event(s)/Activities This Month & Why

My Least Favorite Networking Event(s)/Activities This Month & Why

Goals Accomplished; Major Tasks Completed

Lessons Learned

Monthly Net-Connecting Calendar

Month _____ Year _____

Sunday	Monday	Tuesday	Wednesday	Thursday	Friday	Saturday

Quote/Scripture of the Month

Theme For This Month's Net-Connecting Activities

Monthly Event Summary & Recap

Month _____ Year _____

Total # of Events Attended This Month

Total Spent	Week 1	Week 2	Week 3	Week 4		Total
Planned Monthly Budget $	$				=	$
		Is Total Under Planned Budget?		Is Total Over Planned Budget?		

Key Contacts I Met This Month

Followed Up?

My Favorite Networking Event(s)/Activities This Month & Why

My Least Favorite Networking Event(s)/Activities This Month & Why

Goals Accomplished; Major Tasks Completed

Lessons Learned

Monthly Net-Connecting Calendar

Month _____   Year _____

Sunday	Monday	Tuesday	Wednesday	Thursday	Friday	Saturday

Quote/Scripture of the Month

Theme For This Month's Net-Connecting Activities

Monthly Event Summary & Recap

Month _____ Year _____

Total # of Events Attended This Month

Total Spent	Week 1	Week 2	Week 3	Week 4		Total
Planned Monthly Budget $	$				=	$
		Is Total Under Planned Budget?		Is Total Over Planned Budget?		

Key Contacts I Met This Month

Followed Up?

My Favorite Networking Event(s)/Activities This Month & Why

My Least Favorite Networking Event(s)/Activities This Month & Why

Goals Accomplished; Major Tasks Completed

Lessons Learned

Monthly Net-Connecting Calendar

Month _____   Year _____

Sunday	Monday	Tuesday	Wednesday	Thursday	Friday	Saturday

Quote/Scripture of the Month

Theme For This Month's Net-Connecting Activities

Monthly Event Summary & Recap

Month _____ Year _____

Total # of Events Attended This Month

Total Spent	Week 1	Week 2	Week 3	Week 4		Total
Planned Monthly Budget $	$				=	$
		Is Total Under Planned Budget?		Is Total Over Planned Budget?		

Key Contacts I Met This Month   Followed Up?

My Favorite Networking Event(s)/Activities This Month & Why

My Least Favorite Networking Event(s)/Activities This Month & Why

Goals Accomplished; Major Tasks Completed

Lessons Learned

Part 6

Past Event Summaries

This section allows you to capture a high level summary of events you've attended.
It is meant to act as a quick reference guide to keep track of past events with a few details about the event including whether or not you'd attend again

Past Event Summaries

Event Name

Does event **cost**? Yes No

If yes, how much? $

Event Frequency:

Annual Monthly Weekly

Location (City)

Date(s) I Attended This Event

Event Host/Sponsor

Notes (How did you find out about the event? Would you go again? What did you like about the event? Would you refer others? Write other details you'd like to remember.

Event Name

Event Host/Sponsor

Notes (How did you find out about the event? Would you go again? What did you like about the event? Would you refer others? Write other details you'd like to remember.

Event Cost

Does event **cost**? Yes No

If yes, how much? $

Event Frequency:

Annual Monthly Weekly

Location (City)

Date(s) I Attended This Event

Event Name

Does event **cost**? Yes No

If yes, how much? $

Event Frequency:

Annual Monthly Weekly

Location (City)

Date(s) I Attended This Event

Event Host/Sponsor

Notes (How did you find out about the event? Would you go again? What did you like about the event? Would you refer others? Write other details you'd like to remember.

Event Name

Event Host/Sponsor

Notes (How did you find out about the event? Would you go again? What did you like about the event? Would you refer others? Write other details you'd like to remember.

Event Cost

Does event **cost**? Yes No

If yes, how much? $

Event Frequency:

Annual Monthly Weekly

Location (City)

Date(s) I Attended This Event

Past Event Summaries

Event Name

Does event **cost**?   Yes   No

If yes, how much? $

Event Host/Sponsor

Event Frequency:

Annual   Monthly   Weekly

Location (City)

Notes (How did you find out about the event? Would you go again? What did you like about the event? Would you refer others? Write other details you'd like to remember.

Date(s) I Attended This Event

Event Name

Event Host/Sponsor

Notes (How did you find out about the event? Would you go again? What did you like about the event? Would you refer others? Write other details you'd like to remember.

Event Cost

Does event **cost**?   Yes   No

If yes, how much? $

Event Frequency:

Annual   Monthly   Weekly

Location (City)

Date(s) I Attended This Event

Event Name

Does event **cost**?   Yes   No

If yes, how much? $

Event Frequency:

Annual   Monthly   Weekly

Location (City)

Date(s) I Attended This Event

Event Host/Sponsor

Notes (How did you find out about the event? Would you go again? What did you like about the event? Would you refer others? Write other details you'd like to remember.

Event Name

Event Host/Sponsor

Notes (How did you find out about the event? Would you go again? What did you like about the event? Would you refer others? Write other details you'd like to remember.

Event Cost

Does event **cost**?   Yes   No

If yes, how much? $

Event Frequency:

Annual   Monthly   Weekly

Location (City)

Date(s) I Attended This Event

Past Event Summaries

Event Name

Does event **cost**?   Yes   No

If yes, how much? $

Event Frequency:

Annual   Monthly   Weekly

Location (City)

Date(s) I Attended This Event

Event Host/Sponsor

Notes (How did you find out about the event? Would you go again? What did you like about the event? Would you refer others? Write other details you'd like to remember.

Event Name

Event Host/Sponsor

Notes (How did you find out about the event? Would you go again? What did you like about the event? Would you refer others? Write other details you'd like to remember.

Event Cost

Does event **cost**?   Yes   No

If yes, how much? $

Event Frequency:

Annual   Monthly   Weekly

Location (City)

Date(s) I Attended This Event

Event Name

Does event **cost**?   Yes   No

If yes, how much? $

Event Frequency:

Annual   Monthly   Weekly

Location (City)

Date(s) I Attended This Event

Event Host/Sponsor

Notes (How did you find out about the event? Would you go again? What did you like about the event? Would you refer others? Write other details you'd like to remember.

Event Name

Event Host/Sponsor

Notes (How did you find out about the event? Would you go again? What did you like about the event? Would you refer others? Write other details you'd like to remember.

Event Cost

Does event **cost**?   Yes   No

If yes, how much? $

Event Frequency:

Annual   Monthly   Weekly

Location (City)

Date(s) I Attended This Event

Past Event Summaries

Event Name

Does event **cost**?   Yes   No

If yes, how much? $

Event Frequency:

Annual   Monthly   Weekly

Location (City)

Notes (How did you find out about the event? Would you go again? What did you like about the event? Would you refer others? Write other details you'd like to remember.

Date(s) I Attended This Event

Event Name

Event Host/Sponsor

Notes (How did you find out about the event? Would you go again? What did you like about the event? Would you refer others? Write other details you'd like to remember.

Event Cost

Does event **cost**?   Yes   No

If yes, how much? $

Event Frequency:

Annual   Monthly   Weekly

Location (City)

Date(s) I Attended This Event

Event Name

Does event **cost**?   Yes   No

If yes, how much? $

Event Frequency:

Annual   Monthly   Weekly

Location (City)

Event Host/Sponsor

Notes (How did you find out about the event? Would you go again? What did you like about the event? Would you refer others? Write other details you'd like to remember.

Date(s) I Attended This Event

Event Name

Event Host/Sponsor

Notes (How did you find out about the event? Would you go again? What did you like about the event? Would you refer others? Write other details you'd like to remember.

Event Cost

Does event **cost**?   Yes   No

If yes, how much? $

Event Frequency:

Annual   Monthly   Weekly

Location (City)

Date(s) I Attended This Event

Past Event Summaries

Event Name

Does event **cost**?   Yes   No

If yes, how much? $

Event Frequency:

Annual   Monthly   Weekly

Event Host/Sponsor

Location (City)

Notes (How did you find out about the event? Would you go again? What did you like about the event? Would you refer others? Write other details you'd like to remember.

Date(s) I Attended This Event

Event Name

Event Host/Sponsor

Notes (How did you find out about the event? Would you go again? What did you like about the event? Would you refer others? Write other details you'd like to remember.

Event Cost

Does event **cost**?   Yes   No

If yes, how much? $

Event Frequency:

Annual   Monthly   Weekly

Location (City)

Date(s) I Attended This Event

Event Name

Does event **cost**?   Yes   No

If yes, how much? $

Event Frequency:

Annual   Monthly   Weekly

Event Host/Sponsor

Location (City)

Notes (How did you find out about the event? Would you go again? What did you like about the event? Would you refer others? Write other details you'd like to remember.

Date(s) I Attended This Event

Event Name

Event Host/Sponsor

Notes (How did you find out about the event? Would you go again? What did you like about the event? Would you refer others? Write other details you'd like to remember.

Event Cost

Does event **cost**?   Yes   No

If yes, how much? $

Event Frequency:

Annual   Monthly   Weekly

Location (City)

Date(s) I Attended This Event

Past Event Summaries

Event Name

Does event **cost**?   Yes   No

If yes, how much? $

Event Frequency:

Annual   Monthly   Weekly

Location (City)

Event Host/Sponsor

Notes (How did you find out about the event? Would you go again? What did you like about the event? Would you refer others? Write other details you'd like to remember.

Date(s) I Attended This Event

Event Name

Event Host/Sponsor

Notes (How did you find out about the event? Would you go again? What did you like about the event? Would you refer others? Write other details you'd like to remember.

Event Cost

Does event **cost**?   Yes   No

If yes, how much? $

Event Frequency:

Annual   Monthly   Weekly

Location (City)

Date(s) I Attended This Event

Event Name

Does event **cost**?   Yes   No

If yes, how much? $

Event Frequency:

Annual   Monthly   Weekly

Location (City)

Event Host/Sponsor

Notes (How did you find out about the event? Would you go again? What did you like about the event? Would you refer others? Write other details you'd like to remember.

Date(s) I Attended This Event

Event Name

Event Host/Sponsor

Notes (How did you find out about the event? Would you go again? What did you like about the event? Would you refer others? Write other details you'd like to remember.

Event Cost

Does event **cost**?   Yes   No

If yes, how much? $

Event Frequency:

Annual   Monthly   Weekly

Location (City)

Date(s) I Attended This Event

Past Event Summaries

Event Name

Does event **cost**? Yes No

If yes, how much? $

Event Frequency:

Annual Monthly Weekly

Location (City)

Date(s) I Attended This Event

Notes (How did you find out about the event? Would you go again? What did you like about the event? Would you refer others? Write other details you'd like to remember.

Event Name

Event Host/Sponsor

Notes (How did you find out about the event? Would you go again? What did you like about the event? Would you refer others? Write other details you'd like to remember.

Event Cost

Does event **cost**? Yes No

If yes, how much? $

Event Frequency:

Annual Monthly Weekly

Location (City)

Date(s) I Attended This Event

Event Name

Does event **cost**? Yes No

If yes, how much? $

Event Frequency:

Annual Monthly Weekly

Location (City)

Date(s) I Attended This Event

Event Host/Sponsor

Notes (How did you find out about the event? Would you go again? What did you like about the event? Would you refer others? Write other details you'd like to remember.

Event Name

Event Host/Sponsor

Notes (How did you find out about the event? Would you go again? What did you like about the event? Would you refer others? Write other details you'd like to remember.

Event Cost

Does event **cost**? Yes No

If yes, how much? $

Event Frequency:

Annual Monthly Weekly

Location (City)

Date(s) I Attended This Event

Past Event Summaries

Event Name

Does event **cost**?   Yes   No

If yes, how much? $

Event Frequency:

Annual   Monthly   Weekly

Location (City)

Event Host/Sponsor

Notes (How did you find out about the event? Would you go again? What did you like about the event? Would you refer others? Write other details you'd like to remember.

Date(s) I Attended This Event

Event Name

Event Host/Sponsor

Notes (How did you find out about the event? Would you go again? What did you like about the event? Would you refer others? Write other details you'd like to remember.

Event Cost

Does event **cost**?   Yes   No

If yes, how much? $

Event Frequency:

Annual   Monthly   Weekly

Location (City)

Date(s) I Attended This Event

Event Name

Does event **cost**?   Yes   No

If yes, how much? $

Event Frequency:

Annual   Monthly   Weekly

Location (City)

Date(s) I Attended This Event

Event Host/Sponsor

Notes (How did you find out about the event? Would you go again? What did you like about the event? Would you refer others? Write other details you'd like to remember.

Event Name

Event Host/Sponsor

Notes (How did you find out about the event? Would you go again? What did you like about the event? Would you refer others? Write other details you'd like to remember.

Event Cost

Does event **cost**?   Yes   No

If yes, how much? $

Event Frequency:

Annual   Monthly   Weekly

Location (City)

Date(s) I Attended This Event

Past Event Summaries

Event Name

Does event **cost**?   Yes   No

If yes, how much? $

Event Frequency:

Annual   Monthly   Weekly

Location (City)

Date(s) I Attended This Event

Event Host/Sponsor

Notes (How did you find out about the event? Would you go again? What did you like about the event? Would you refer others? Write other details you'd like to remember.

Event Name

Event Host/Sponsor

Notes (How did you find out about the event? Would you go again? What did you like about the event? Would you refer others? Write other details you'd like to remember.

Event Cost

Does event **cost**?   Yes   No

If yes, how much? $

Event Frequency:

Annual   Monthly   Weekly

Location (City)

Date(s) I Attended This Event

Event Name

Does event **cost**?   Yes   No

If yes, how much? $

Event Frequency:

Annual   Monthly   Weekly

Location (City)

Date(s) I Attended This Event

Event Host/Sponsor

Notes (How did you find out about the event? Would you go again? What did you like about the event? Would you refer others? Write other details you'd like to remember.

Event Name

Event Host/Sponsor

Notes (How did you find out about the event? Would you go again? What did you like about the event? Would you refer others? Write other details you'd like to remember.

Event Cost

Does event **cost**?   Yes   No

If yes, how much? $

Event Frequency:

Annual   Monthly   Weekly

Location (City)

Date(s) I Attended This Event

Past Event Summaries

Event Name

Does event **cost**?   Yes   No

If yes, how much? $

Event Frequency:

Annual   Monthly   Weekly

Location (City)

Event Host/Sponsor

Notes (How did you find out about the event? Would you go again? What did you like about the event? Would you refer others? Write other details you'd like to remember.

Date(s) I Attended This Event

Event Name

Event Host/Sponsor

Notes (How did you find out about the event? Would you go again? What did you like about the event? Would you refer others? Write other details you'd like to remember.

Event Cost

Does event **cost**?   Yes   No

If yes, how much? $

Event Frequency:

Annual   Monthly   Weekly

Location (City)

Date(s) I Attended This Event

Event Name

Does event **cost**?   Yes   No

If yes, how much? $

Event Frequency:

Annual   Monthly   Weekly

Location (City)

Event Host/Sponsor

Notes (How did you find out about the event? Would you go again? What did you like about the event? Would you refer others? Write other details you'd like to remember.

Date(s) I Attended This Event

Event Name

Event Host/Sponsor

Notes (How did you find out about the event? Would you go again? What did you like about the event? Would you refer others? Write other details you'd like to remember.

Event Cost

Does event **cost**?   Yes   No

If yes, how much? $

Event Frequency:

Annual   Monthly   Weekly

Location (City)

Date(s) I Attended This Event

Past Event Summaries

Event Name

Does event **cost**?   Yes   No

If yes, how much? $

Event Frequency:

Annual   Monthly   Weekly

Location (City)

Event Host/Sponsor

Notes (How did you find out about the event? Would you go again? What did you like about the event? Would you refer others? Write other details you'd like to remember.

Date(s) I Attended This Event

Event Name

Event Host/Sponsor

Notes (How did you find out about the event? Would you go again? What did you like about the event? Would you refer others? Write other details you'd like to remember.

Event Cost

Does event **cost**?   Yes   No

If yes, how much? $

Event Frequency:

Annual   Monthly   Weekly

Location (City)

Date(s) I Attended This Event

Event Name

Does event **cost**?   Yes   No

If yes, how much? $

Event Frequency:

Annual   Monthly   Weekly

Location (City)

Event Host/Sponsor

Notes (How did you find out about the event? Would you go again? What did you like about the event? Would you refer others? Write other details you'd like to remember.

Date(s) I Attended This Event

Event Name

Event Host/Sponsor

Notes (How did you find out about the event? Would you go again? What did you like about the event? Would you refer others? Write other details you'd like to remember.

Event Cost

Does event **cost**?   Yes   No

If yes, how much? $

Event Frequency:

Annual   Monthly   Weekly

Location (City)

Date(s) I Attended This Event

Past Event Summaries

Event Name

Does event **cost**?   Yes   No

If yes, how much? $

Event Frequency:

Annual   Monthly   Weekly

Location (City)

Date(s) I Attended This Event

Notes (How did you find out about the event? Would you go again? What did you like about the event? Would you refer others? Write other details you'd like to remember.

Event Name

Event Host/Sponsor

Notes (How did you find out about the event? Would you go again? What did you like about the event? Would you refer others? Write other details you'd like to remember.

Event Cost

Does event **cost**?   Yes   No

If yes, how much? $

Event Frequency:

Annual   Monthly   Weekly

Location (City)

Date(s) I Attended This Event

Event Name

Does event **cost**?   Yes   No

If yes, how much? $

Event Frequency:

Annual   Monthly   Weekly

Location (City)

Date(s) I Attended This Event

Event Host/Sponsor

Notes (How did you find out about the event? Would you go again? What did you like about the event? Would you refer others? Write other details you'd like to remember.

Event Name

Event Host/Sponsor

Notes (How did you find out about the event? Would you go again? What did you like about the event? Would you refer others? Write other details you'd like to remember.

Event Cost

Does event **cost**?   Yes   No

If yes, how much? $

Event Frequency:

Annual   Monthly   Weekly

Location (City)

Date(s) I Attended This Event

Past Event Summaries

Event Name

Does event **cost**?   Yes   No

If yes, how much? $

Event Frequency:

Annual   Monthly   Weekly

Event Host/Sponsor

Location (City)

Notes (How did you find out about the event? Would you go again? What did you like about the event? Would you refer others? Write other details you'd like to remember.

Date(s) I Attended This Event

Event Name

Event Host/Sponsor

Notes (How did you find out about the event? Would you go again? What did you like about the event? Would you refer others? Write other details you'd like to remember.

Event Cost

Does event **cost**?   Yes   No

If yes, how much? $

Event Frequency:

Annual   Monthly   Weekly

Location (City)

Date(s) I Attended This Event

Event Name

Does event **cost**?   Yes   No

If yes, how much? $

Event Frequency:

Annual   Monthly   Weekly

Event Host/Sponsor

Location (City)

Notes (How did you find out about the event? Would you go again? What did you like about the event? Would you refer others? Write other details you'd like to remember.

Date(s) I Attended This Event

Event Name

Event Host/Sponsor

Notes (How did you find out about the event? Would you go again? What did you like about the event? Would you refer others? Write other details you'd like to remember.

Event Cost

Does event **cost**?   Yes   No

If yes, how much? $

Event Frequency:

Annual   Monthly   Weekly

Location (City)

Date(s) I Attended This Event

Past Event Summaries

Event Name

Does event **cost**?   Yes   No

If yes, how much? $

Event Frequency:

Annual   Monthly   Weekly

Location (City)

Notes (How did you find out about the event? Would you go again? What did you like about the event? Would you refer others? Write other details you'd like to remember.

Date(s) I Attended This Event

Event Name

Event Host/Sponsor

Notes (How did you find out about the event? Would you go again? What did you like about the event? Would you refer others? Write other details you'd like to remember.

Event Cost

Does event **cost**?   Yes   No

If yes, how much? $

Event Frequency:

Annual   Monthly   Weekly

Location (City)

Date(s) I Attended This Event

Event Name

Does event **cost**?   Yes   No

If yes, how much? $

Event Frequency:

Annual   Monthly   Weekly

Location (City)

Event Host/Sponsor

Notes (How did you find out about the event? Would you go again? What did you like about the event? Would you refer others? Write other details you'd like to remember.

Date(s) I Attended This Event

Event Name

Event Host/Sponsor

Notes (How did you find out about the event? Would you go again? What did you like about the event? Would you refer others? Write other details you'd like to remember.

Event Cost

Does event **cost**?   Yes   No

If yes, how much? $

Event Frequency:

Annual   Monthly   Weekly

Location (City)

Date(s) I Attended This Event

Past Event Summaries

Event Name

Does event **cost**? Yes No

If yes, how much? $

Event Frequency:

Annual   Monthly   Weekly

Location (City)

Event Host/Sponsor

Notes (How did you find out about the event? Would you go again? What did you like about the event? Would you refer others? Write other details you'd like to remember.

Date(s) I Attended This Event

Event Name

Event Host/Sponsor

Notes (How did you find out about the event? Would you go again? What did you like about the event? Would you refer others? Write other details you'd like to remember.

Event Cost

Does event **cost**? Yes No

If yes, how much? $

Event Frequency:

Annual   Monthly   Weekly

Location (City)

Date(s) I Attended This Event

Event Name

Does event **cost**? Yes No

If yes, how much? $

Event Frequency:

Annual   Monthly   Weekly

Location (City)

Event Host/Sponsor

Notes (How did you find out about the event? Would you go again? What did you like about the event? Would you refer others? Write other details you'd like to remember.

Date(s) I Attended This Event

Event Name

Event Host/Sponsor

Notes (How did you find out about the event? Would you go again? What did you like about the event? Would you refer others? Write other details you'd like to remember.

Event Cost

Does event **cost**? Yes No

If yes, how much? $

Event Frequency:

Annual   Monthly   Weekly

Location (City)

Date(s) I Attended This Event

Part 7

My Power Moves

This is the section where you will keep up with your POWER MOVES as the book describes. There are specific details you can capture for each contact that will be helpful as you build your network.

My Power Moves

Code   Name   Follow Up Date

Company (If applicable)   Phone/Text

Where/How We Met/Referred   Reason for Contact?

Outcome of Follow-Up / Action Items

Linkedin   Instagram   Twitter

Other Social Media or Website   Facebook

Code   Name   Follow Up Date

Company (If applicable)   Phone/Text

Where/How We Met/Referred   Reason for Contact?

Outcome of Follow-Up / Action Items

Linkedin   Instagram   Twitter

Other Social Media or Website   Facebook

Code   Name   Follow Up Date

Company (If applicable)   Phone/Text

Where/How We Met/Referred   Reason for Contact?

Outcome of Follow-Up / Action Items

Linkedin   Instagram   Twitter

Other Social Media or Website   Facebook

My Power Moves

Code   Name   Follow Up Date

Company (If applicable)   Phone/Text

Where/How We Met/Referred   Reason for Contact?

Outcome of Follow-Up / Action Items

Linkedin   Instagram   Twitter

Other Social Media or Website   Facebook

Code   Name   Follow Up Date

Company (If applicable)   Phone/Text

Where/How We Met/Referred   Reason for Contact?

Outcome of Follow-Up / Action Items

Linkedin   Instagram   Twitter

Other Social Media or Website   Facebook

Code   Name   Follow Up Date

Company (If applicable)   Phone/Text

Where/How We Met/Referred   Reason for Contact?

Outcome of Follow-Up / Action Items

Linkedin   Instagram   Twitter

Other Social Media or Website   Facebook

My Power Moves

Code   Name   Follow Up Date

Company (If applicable)   Phone/Text

Where/How We Met/Referred   Reason for Contact?

Outcome of Follow-Up / Action Items

Linkedin   Instagram   Twitter

Other Social Media or Website   Facebook

Code   Name   Follow Up Date

Company (If applicable)   Phone/Text

Where/How We Met/Referred   Reason for Contact?

Outcome of Follow-Up / Action Items

Linkedin   Instagram   Twitter

Other Social Media or Website   Facebook

Code   Name   Follow Up Date

Company (If applicable)   Phone/Text

Where/How We Met/Referred   Reason for Contact?

Outcome of Follow-Up / Action Items

Linkedin   Instagram   Twitter

Other Social Media or Website   Facebook

My Power Moves

Code   Name

Follow Up Date

Company (If applicable)

Phone/Text

Where/How We Met/Referred

Reason for Contact?

Outcome of Follow-Up / Action Items

Linkedin

Instagram

Twitter

Other Social Media or Website

Facebook

Code   Name

Follow Up Date

Company (If applicable)

Phone/Text

Where/How We Met/Referred

Reason for Contact?

Outcome of Follow-Up / Action Items

Linkedin

Instagram

Twitter

Other Social Media or Website

Facebook

Code   Name

Follow Up Date

Company (If applicable)

Phone/Text

Where/How We Met/Referred

Reason for Contact?

Outcome of Follow-Up / Action Items

Linkedin

Instagram

Twitter

Other Social Media or Website

Facebook

My Power Moves

Code   Name   Follow Up Date

Company (If applicable)   Phone/Text

Where/How We Met/Referred   Reason for Contact?

Outcome of Follow-Up / Action Items

Linkedin   Instagram   Twitter

Other Social Media or Website   Facebook

Code   Name   Follow Up Date

Company (If applicable)   Phone/Text

Where/How We Met/Referred   Reason for Contact?

Outcome of Follow-Up / Action Items

Linkedin   Instagram   Twitter

Other Social Media or Website   Facebook

Code   Name   Follow Up Date

Company (If applicable)   Phone/Text

Where/How We Met/Referred   Reason for Contact?

Outcome of Follow-Up / Action Items

Linkedin   Instagram   Twitter

Other Social Media or Website   Facebook

My Power Moves

Code   Name   Follow Up Date

Company (If applicable)   Phone/Text

Where/How We Met/Referred   Reason for Contact?

Outcome of Follow-Up / Action Items

Linkedin   Instagram   Twitter

Other Social Media or Website   Facebook

Code   Name   Follow Up Date

Company (If applicable)   Phone/Text

Where/How We Met/Referred   Reason for Contact?

Outcome of Follow-Up / Action Items

Linkedin   Instagram   Twitter

Other Social Media or Website   Facebook

Code   Name   Follow Up Date

Company (If applicable)   Phone/Text

Where/How We Met/Referred   Reason for Contact?

Outcome of Follow-Up / Action Items

Linkedin   Instagram   Twitter

Other Social Media or Website   Facebook

My Power Moves

Code   Name   Follow Up Date

Company (If applicable)   Phone/Text

Where/How We Met/Referred   Reason for Contact?

Outcome of Follow-Up / Action Items

Linkedin   Instagram   Twitter

Other Social Media or Website   Facebook

Code   Name   Follow Up Date

Company (If applicable)   Phone/Text

Where/How We Met/Referred   Reason for Contact?

Outcome of Follow-Up / Action Items

Linkedin   Instagram   Twitter

Other Social Media or Website   Facebook

Code   Name   Follow Up Date

Company (If applicable)   Phone/Text

Where/How We Met/Referred   Reason for Contact?

Outcome of Follow-Up / Action Items

Linkedin   Instagram   Twitter

Other Social Media or Website   Facebook

My Power Moves

Code   Name

Follow Up Date

Company (If applicable)

Phone/Text

Where/How We Met/Referred

Reason for Contact?

Outcome of Follow-Up / Action Items

Linkedin

Instagram

Twitter

Other Social Media or Website

Facebook

Code   Name

Follow Up Date

Company (If applicable)

Phone/Text

Where/How We Met/Referred

Reason for Contact?

Outcome of Follow-Up / Action Items

Linkedin

Instagram

Twitter

Other Social Media or Website

Facebook

Code   Name

Follow Up Date

Company (If applicable)

Phone/Text

Where/How We Met/Referred

Reason for Contact?

Outcome of Follow-Up / Action Items

Linkedin

Instagram

Twitter

Other Social Media or Website

Facebook

My Power Moves

Code   Name   Follow Up Date

Company (If applicable)   Phone/Text

Where/How We Met/Referred   Reason for Contact?

Outcome of Follow-Up / Action Items

Linkedin   Instagram   Twitter

Other Social Media or Website   Facebook

Code   Name   Follow Up Date

Company (If applicable)   Phone/Text

Where/How We Met/Referred   Reason for Contact?

Outcome of Follow-Up / Action Items

Linkedin   Instagram   Twitter

Other Social Media or Website   Facebook

Code   Name   Follow Up Date

Company (If applicable)   Phone/Text

Where/How We Met/Referred   Reason for Contact?

Outcome of Follow-Up / Action Items

Linkedin   Instagram   Twitter

Other Social Media or Website   Facebook

My Power Moves

Code   Name   Follow Up Date

Company (If applicable)   Phone/Text

Where/How We Met/Referred   Reason for Contact?

Outcome of Follow-Up / Action Items

Linkedin   Instagram   Twitter

Other Social Media or Website   Facebook

Code   Name   Follow Up Date

Company (If applicable)   Phone/Text

Where/How We Met/Referred   Reason for Contact?

Outcome of Follow-Up / Action Items

Linkedin   Instagram   Twitter

Other Social Media or Website   Facebook

Code   Name   Follow Up Date

Company (If applicable)   Phone/Text

Where/How We Met/Referred   Reason for Contact?

Outcome of Follow-Up / Action Items

Linkedin   Instagram   Twitter

Other Social Media or Website   Facebook

My Power Moves

Code   Name   Follow Up Date

Company (If applicable)   Phone/Text

Where/How We Met/Referred   Reason for Contact?

Outcome of Follow-Up / Action Items

Linkedin   Instagram   Twitter

Other Social Media or Website   Facebook

Code   Name   Follow Up Date

Company (If applicable)   Phone/Text

Where/How We Met/Referred   Reason for Contact?

Outcome of Follow-Up / Action Items

Linkedin   Instagram   Twitter

Other Social Media or Website   Facebook

Code   Name   Follow Up Date

Company (If applicable)   Phone/Text

Where/How We Met/Referred   Reason for Contact?

Outcome of Follow-Up / Action Items

Linkedin   Instagram   Twitter

Other Social Media or Website   Facebook

My Power Moves

Code   Name   Follow Up Date

Company (If applicable)   Phone/Text

Where/How We Met/Referred   Reason for Contact?

Outcome of Follow-Up / Action Items

Linkedin   Instagram   Twitter

Other Social Media or Website   Facebook

Code   Name   Follow Up Date

Company (If applicable)   Phone/Text

Where/How We Met/Referred   Reason for Contact?

Outcome of Follow-Up / Action Items

Linkedin   Instagram   Twitter

Other Social Media or Website   Facebook

Code   Name   Follow Up Date

Company (If applicable)   Phone/Text

Where/How We Met/Referred   Reason for Contact?

Outcome of Follow-Up / Action Items

Linkedin   Instagram   Twitter

Other Social Media or Website   Facebook

My Power Moves

Code   Name   Follow Up Date

Company (If applicable)   Phone/Text

Where/How We Met/Referred   Reason for Contact?

Outcome of Follow-Up / Action Items

Linkedin   Instagram   Twitter

Other Social Media or Website   Facebook

Code   Name   Follow Up Date

Company (If applicable)   Phone/Text

Where/How We Met/Referred   Reason for Contact?

Outcome of Follow-Up / Action Items

Linkedin   Instagram   Twitter

Other Social Media or Website   Facebook

Code   Name   Follow Up Date

Company (If applicable)   Phone/Text

Where/How We Met/Referred   Reason for Contact?

Outcome of Follow-Up / Action Items

Linkedin   Instagram   Twitter

Other Social Media or Website   Facebook

My Power Moves

Code   Name

Follow Up Date

Company (If applicable)

Phone/Text

Where/How We Met/Referred   Reason for Contact?

Outcome of Follow-Up / Action Items

Linkedin   Instagram   Twitter

Other Social Media or Website   Facebook

Code   Name

Follow Up Date

Company (If applicable)

Phone/Text

Where/How We Met/Referred   Reason for Contact?

Outcome of Follow-Up / Action Items

Linkedin   Instagram   Twitter

Other Social Media or Website   Facebook

Code   Name

Follow Up Date

Company (If applicable)

Phone/Text

Where/How We Met/Referred   Reason for Contact?

Outcome of Follow-Up / Action Items

Linkedin   Instagram   Twitter

Other Social Media or Website   Facebook

My Power Moves

Code   Name   Follow Up Date

Company (If applicable)   Phone/Text

Where/How We Met/Referred   Reason for Contact?

Outcome of Follow-Up / Action Items

Linkedin   Instagram   Twitter

Other Social Media or Website   Facebook

Code   Name   Follow Up Date

Company (If applicable)   Phone/Text

Where/How We Met/Referred   Reason for Contact?

Outcome of Follow-Up / Action Items

Linkedin   Instagram   Twitter

Other Social Media or Website   Facebook

Code   Name   Follow Up Date

Company (If applicable)   Phone/Text

Where/How We Met/Referred   Reason for Contact?

Outcome of Follow-Up / Action Items

Linkedin   Instagram   Twitter

Other Social Media or Website   Facebook

My Power Moves

Code   Name

Follow Up Date

Company (If applicable)

Phone/Text

Where/How We Met/Referred   Reason for Contact?

Outcome of Follow-Up / Action Items

Linkedin   Instagram   Twitter

Other Social Media or Website   Facebook

Code   Name

Follow Up Date

Company (If applicable)

Phone/Text

Where/How We Met/Referred   Reason for Contact?

Outcome of Follow-Up / Action Items

Linkedin   Instagram   Twitter

Other Social Media or Website   Facebook

Code   Name

Follow Up Date

Company (If applicable)

Phone/Text

Where/How We Met/Referred   Reason for Contact?

Outcome of Follow-Up / Action Items

Linkedin   Instagram   Twitter

Other Social Media or Website   Facebook

My Power Moves

Code   Name   Follow Up Date

Company (If applicable)   Phone/Text

Where/How We Met/Referred   Reason for Contact?

Outcome of Follow-Up / Action Items

Linkedin   Instagram   Twitter

Other Social Media or Website   Facebook

Code   Name   Follow Up Date

Company (If applicable)   Phone/Text

Where/How We Met/Referred   Reason for Contact?

Outcome of Follow-Up / Action Items

Linkedin   Instagram   Twitter

Other Social Media or Website   Facebook

Code   Name   Follow Up Date

Company (If applicable)   Phone/Text

Where/How We Met/Referred   Reason for Contact?

Outcome of Follow-Up / Action Items

Linkedin   Instagram   Twitter

Other Social Media or Website   Facebook

My Power Moves

Code   Name   Follow Up Date

Company (If applicable)   Phone/Text

Where/How We Met/Referred   Reason for Contact?

Outcome of Follow-Up / Action Items

Linkedin   Instagram   Twitter

Other Social Media or Website   Facebook

Code   Name   Follow Up Date

Company (If applicable)   Phone/Text

Where/How We Met/Referred   Reason for Contact?

Outcome of Follow-Up / Action Items

Linkedin   Instagram   Twitter

Other Social Media or Website   Facebook

Code   Name   Follow Up Date

Company (If applicable)   Phone/Text

Where/How We Met/Referred   Reason for Contact?

Outcome of Follow-Up / Action Items

Linkedin   Instagram   Twitter

Other Social Media or Website   Facebook

My Power Moves

Code   Name   Follow Up Date

Company (If applicable)   Phone/Text

Where/How We Met/Referred   Reason for Contact?

Outcome of Follow-Up / Action Items

Linkedin   Instagram   Twitter

Other Social Media or Website   Facebook

Code   Name   Follow Up Date

Company (If applicable)   Phone/Text

Where/How We Met/Referred   Reason for Contact?

Outcome of Follow-Up / Action Items

Linkedin   Instagram   Twitter

Other Social Media or Website   Facebook

Code   Name   Follow Up Date

Company (If applicable)   Phone/Text

Where/How We Met/Referred   Reason for Contact?

Outcome of Follow-Up / Action Items

Linkedin   Instagram   Twitter

Other Social Media or Website   Facebook

My Power Moves

Code   Name   Follow Up Date

Company (If applicable)   Phone/Text

Where/How We Met/Referred   Reason for Contact?

Outcome of Follow-Up / Action Items

Linkedin   Instagram   Twitter

Other Social Media or Website   Facebook

Code   Name   Follow Up Date

Company (If applicable)   Phone/Text

Where/How We Met/Referred   Reason for Contact?

Outcome of Follow-Up / Action Items

Linkedin   Instagram   Twitter

Other Social Media or Website   Facebook

Code   Name   Follow Up Date

Company (If applicable)   Phone/Text

Where/How We Met/Referred   Reason for Contact?

Outcome of Follow-Up / Action Items

Linkedin   Instagram   Twitter

Other Social Media or Website   Facebook

Part 8

My Notes

This section is available for you to jot down quick ideas and thoughts as you attend and participate in net-connecting events and activities.

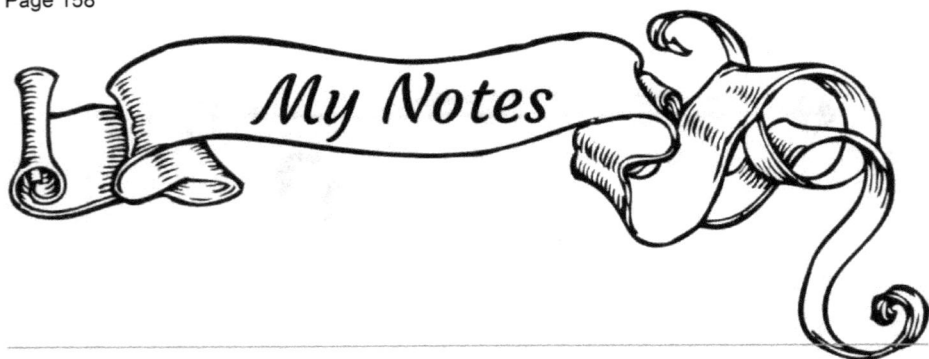

My Notes

My Notes

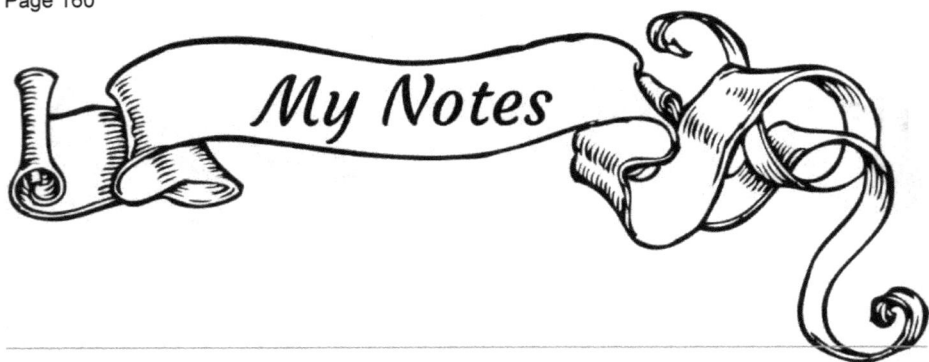

My Notes

My Notes

My Notes

My Notes

My Notes